Easy Vegan Recipes for Kids

A simple guide to vegan cooking that even your children will love.

Tyler Buckhouse

Table of Contents

Easy Vegan Recipes for Kids

For parents who have embraced the vegan movement, it is always tough to make your kids eat whatever you are serving for your meals.

We all know how that conversation usually goes. You serve something that doesn't catch your kids' attention and they'll barely touch their food. At the very worst, they'll have tantrums or even leave the table in protest. This is especially true if you're running out of ideas how to conceal veggies so that they look less like vegetables and more like something that your kids will love.

The other option of dealing with this is less palatable. The last thing that you want to do is to shop separately for you and your kids. That means cooking your own meals and cooking something different for your kids. That's double the effort and a stark departure from the reasons that you became a vegan.

What can you do about this situation? You can try reasoning with your kids but more often than not, that will not get you anywhere. Take broccoli as an example; no matter how much you tell them that it's good, you will always encounter some level of resistance that will lead to disagreements and drama episodes at the kitchen table.

I wrote this book to help you deal with your meal problems.

You will find recipes that are specifically chosen because I know your kids will love them. Just because you've gone vegan doesn't mean you can't make great dishes that will convince your kids that veggies can taste great too. Your kids won't ask what's in their food if they already love it just by looking at it and having their first bite.

The overall motivation is that a vegan diet can offer tremendous health benefits for your kids.

Consider:

1. Going vegan helps to lower your kids' intake of meat products which is a source of cholesterol and saturated fat. You may have already noticed how many kids are becoming overweight. Cutting meat from their diet – even just partially – can help to improve their daily nutrition drastically.

2. Vegan recipes naturally have a higher amount of vitamins and minerals that are lacking in traditional modern diets. We try to compensate for this fact by giving our kids vitamin supplements. However, there is no substitute for vitamins and minerals from vegetables. By feeding them vegan recipes, you can improve their daily vitamin and mineral intake without having to rely on expensive vitamin supplements.

3. Going vegan, even partially, can help your kids to develop good habits that they will carry into their later years. The adage "you can't teach an old dog new tricks" is particularly

true when it comes to the food we eat. Therefore, teaching your kids to like veggies at a young age will enable them to switch to healthier diets as they grow older. By adding vegan recipes into their diet, you can prepare them for a healthier life than if you were to spoil them with processed foods and sweets.

These might sound like very simple benefits but do not underestimate their value in making a difference in your kids' lives. The following recipes can lead your kids to a healthier lifestyle even at a young age.

30 Easy Vegan Recipes for Kids

Here are 30 kid-friendly and easy vegan recipes that will leave your kids asking for more.

Cookie Dough Balls

These are no-cook cookie dough balls designed to entice your little ones to love bananas, oats, and coconut. For best results, use gluten-free oats and natural sweeteners like maple, agave syrup, or stevia to make it even healthier.

This recipe is a no-bake cookie ball so it makes your life easier while still delivering something that your kids are guaranteed to ask for again.

Yield: 12 cookie balls

Ingredients:

- 1 cup oats
- 1 banana, ripe
- 1 tsp. vanilla extract
- 3 tbsp. maple syrup
- ½ cup vegan chocolate chips
- ½ cup coconut, grated, unsweetened
- 2 tbsp. coconut oil

Instructions:

1. Use a food processor to break down the oats slightly. This should take about 15-25 seconds depending on your food processor.

2. To the partially broken oats, add the rest of the ingredients except for the chocolate chips. Continue pulsing until all of the ingredients are fully combined.

3. Add the chocolate chips and pulse for another 5 seconds to quickly combine the chocolate chips.

4. Test the consistency of the dough. You want it to be firm enough to fold into balls. If the dough is too soft, refrigerate the mixture for about 15 minutes to allow it to harden. Afterwards, roll the dough into balls.

5. Put the rolled dough into the refrigerator for 1 hour before serving.

6. Serve, or store in an airtight container in the refrigerator until you are ready to serve it.

Tortilla Pierogies

Pierogies are a famous Canadian treat. They're little dumplings filled with mashed potatoes and ideal for a carb-rich diet that's still healthy and filling.

This recipe uses flour tortillas so they cook quicker. You can also use vegan sour cream to add a fancy twist to the dish. This dish is simple and yet so flavorful that it's guaranteed to have your kids asking for more.

This will definitely become a crowd favorite.

Yield: 4 pieces

Ingredients:

- 2 small flour tortillas
- 2 small potatoes, scrubbed, peeled, diced
- 1 tsp. vegan margarine
- 1 cup spinach, chopped
- 2 tsp. vegetable oil
- ¼ tsp. white truffle oil
- 1 onion, small, chopped finely
- 1 tbsp. chives, chopped finely
- 2 tbsp. vegan sour cream
- salt
- pepper

Instructions:

1. Cook the potatoes by putting them in a pan with water and allowing the water to boil. Depending on the size of the potatoes, this will take about 15 to 30 minutes. You can confirm that the potatoes are cooked if a fork sticks easily through them. Once done, set the potatoes aside.

2. In a separate pan, heat the vegetable oil and sauté the onions until brown. Toss in the spinach until wilted. Set aside.

3. Mash the potatoes. Put them into a bowl with the margarine. Season with salt and pepper and mash until smooth.

4. In another bowl, mix the vegan sour cream and truffle oil and then set aside.

5. You're now ready to put everything together. On a cutting board, lay down one tortilla and spread the mashed potatoes on top of it. Add the onion and spinach mixture and top off with another tortilla to make a tortilla sandwich.

6. In a frying pan, add a teaspoon of vegetable oil and cook the tortilla for 2 minutes or until brown. Turn over carefully to ensure that the tortilla stays intact.

7. Cut into four pieces and garnish with vegan sour cream and chives.

Quinoa Casserole

This might not look like a conventional dish your kids will love. However, looks can be deceiving. The flavor will be more than enough to sway their opinion. Give it a try and watch them ask for more the next time around.

Yield: 8 pieces

Ingredients:

- 1 cup quinoa, uncooked
- 1 can diced tomatoes, include the liquid
- 1 can corn kernels, liquid included
- 1 can black beans, rinsed, drained
- 3 cups baby spinach
- 1 tbsp. vegetable oil
- 1 onion, chopped
- ½ tsp. chilli powder
- 1 clove garlic, minced
- ½ cup water

- 1 tbsp. tomato paste
- 1 tsp. oregano
- 1 tsp. cumin
- salt and pepper
- toppings of your choice

Instructions

1. Preheat your oven to 350 F.

2. In a pan over medium heat, add one tablespoon of olive oil and then the onion and garlic. Sauté for about 5 minutes or until the onions are translucent. Afterwards, remove from heat and transfer it to an oven-safe casserole dish.

3. To the dish, add the quinoa, water, diced tomatoes, tomato paste and spices. Flavor with salt and pepper and combine thoroughly. Cover the dish and place it in the oven for 30 minutes.

4. After 30 minutes, take out the casserole dish from the oven and add the drained beans and the corn with liquid. If the mixture looks dry, add another half cup of water before covering and returning into the oven for another 30 minutes.

5. Remove the casserole dish from the oven and add the spinach. Top with toppings of your choice. We recommend diced avocados and finely chopped cilantro.

Cauliflower Mash

If you need an alternative to mashed potatoes that your kids will love, this is it. It has to be said that if you don't mash cauliflower properly, it becomes grainy which wouldn't sit well with your kids.

However, if you work the mash properly and flavor it accordingly, there's very little reason that you can't pass this for mashed potatoes and that would be a great meal for your kids on any given day.

Yield: 4 servings

Ingredients:

- 1 large cauliflower, chopped
- 2 tbsp. vegan margarine
- 1 clove garlic
- 1 tbsp. chives, fresh, chopped
- 2 tbsp. nutritional yeast

- salt and pepper

Instructions:

1. Put the cauliflower florets into a large pot and fill with water. Bring the water to a boil and then simmer until the florets are tender. This will take about six minutes.
2. Drain the cauliflower and toss it into a large bowl. Mash using a fork or potato masher. You can also use a blender to produce a smooth, thick mixture.
3. Flavor with the remaining ingredients and serve.

Vegan Orange Juice

This is as simple as it can ever get for you; simply use fresh orange juice blended with bananas to make for an awesome morning drink for your little ones.

Ingredients:

- 1 cup orange juice, fresh
- ½ banana, chopped
- 1 cup ice

Instructions:

1. Mix everything in a blender and serve.

Chocolate Banana Muffins

Here's something that your kids will adore.

These vegan chocolate and banana muffins are for snacks, as packed food for school, or even a whimsical breakfast on a weekend.

The best part is: these muffins are healthy for your kids.

Yield: 6 pieces

Ingredients:

- ¾ cup applesauce (or other egg substitute)
- 2 tbsp. soy yogurt
- 1 tbsp. lemon juice
- 1 ½ cups chickpea flour
- 2 bananas, mashed

- ¾ cup sugar
- ¼ cup cocoa powder
- ½ cup coconut oil
- 1 tsp. baking powder

Instructions:

1. Preheat your oven to 350°F.
2. Whisk the egg replacer together with the sugar until fluffy. Add the coconut oil, soy yogurt, 1 tbsp. lemon juice, and mashed bananas. Stir well until completely mixed.
3. Sift the flour together with the cocoa powder and baking powder. Add this into the batter and mix well.
4. Fill the muffin cups and bake for 25 minutes. Serve hot or cold.

Peanut Butter and Jelly Bars

If your kids like peanut butter and jelly sandwiches, then they'll love this wonderful alternative. Prepare these PB&J bars for dessert or for any occasion.

Yield: 16 bars

Ingredients:

- ¾ cup peanut butter, preferably smooth
- ¾ cup strawberry jelly
- ⅓ cup peanuts, dry-roasted, salted, chopped
- 11/2 tsp. coconut oil, hardened in fridge until the consistency of soft butter
- ¼ applesauce (or other egg substitute)
- ¾ cup brown sugar
- 11/2 cups whole wheat flour
- ½ tsp. baking powder
- ¼ tsp. salt
- 1 tsp. vanilla extract

Instructions:

1. The night before, put ½ tsp. coconut oil in the refrigerator to allow it to harden to the consistency of soft butter.

2. Preheat your oven to 350°F.

3. Line a metal baking pan with foil and make sure to leave a 2-inch overhang around edges. Coat the foil with 1 tsp. coconut oil and set aside.

4. In a small bowl, whisk the flour with the baking powder and salt in a small bowl.

5. In a separate large bowl, use an electric mixer to mix the peanut butter, remaining coconut oil, and sugar. Continue mixing while adding the applesauce and vanilla extract until smooth. Add the flour mixture from the small bowl and continue mixing at low speed.

6. Put half of the dough in the lined pan and the other half in the freezer for about 10 minutes. Make sure to even out the dough at the bottom of the pan so it will cook evenly, then spread the jelly into an even layer. Remove the remaining dough from the freezer and break into half-inch pieces and scatter over the jelly layer. Finish by sprinkling the chopped nuts on top.

7. Bake for about 30 minutes or until the top is golden brown. Allow the bars to cool for about 2 hours before removing from the foil and then cut into 16 pieces. Prepare the bars a few days ahead of time so that it hardens in the refrigerator.

Oatmeal Chip Cookies

Let's face it, who in the world doesn't love a good oatmeal chip cookie? You now have a recipe you can depend on to keep your kids occupied with a cookie or two when you need to get some serious work at home done. Or maybe that's just an excuse; and for sure, no one needs an excuse to snack on great oatmeal chip cookies.

So, enjoy!

Yield: 4-5 dozen cookies

Ingredients:

- 2 cups rolled oats
- 1 cup coconut oil
- ¾ cup brown sugar
- 1 tsp. baking soda
- ¼ cup white sugar
- 1 tsp. vanilla
- 11/2 cups flour
- ½ tsp. salt
- ⅓ cup boiling water

- ½ cup walnuts, chopped
- ¾ cup vegan chocolate chips

Instructions:

1. Put the coconut oil in the refrigerator the night before to allow it to harden to the consistency of soft butter.
2. When you start preparing this dish, beat the coconut oil until it is soft. Add the sugars and continue beating until fluffy, then add the vanilla, flour, and salt. Mix well.
3. In the boiling water, dissolve the baking soda and add to the mixture. Continue stirring in the rolled oats, nuts and chocolate chips.
4. To make the bars, roll the mixture into balls and then flatten with a fork dipped in cold water to prevent the mixture from sticking to the fork. Bake at 350 F for about 10 minutes. Cool down before serving.

Banana-Mango Ice Cream

Who says you can't have ice cream if you're a vegan? There are now plenty of substitutes to dairy productst so making vegan ice cream is no longer a problem. The best part is: this is something that your kids will love. Check out the recipe and make summer come early to your home.

Yield: 6 servings

Ingredients:

For the ice cream:

- 4 bananas, chopped, frozen
- ½ cup mango, chopped, frozen
- ¼ tsp. vanilla bean, ground
- 4 tbsp. agave nectar

Instructions:

1. In a blender or food processor, blend the bananas, vanilla bean, agave nectar and mangoes until smooth. Once you're happy with the consistency, pop it back in the refrigerator for about 15 minutes before serving.

Plum and Apple Crumble

Here's a simple crumble recipe that's perfect for dessert. If your kids love pie, this is a great alternative that you can prepare first and serve anytime that your kids are feeling the craving.

Yield: 6-8 servings

Ingredients:

For the crumble:

- 6 plums (large)
- 2 cooking apples (large)
- pinch of cinnamon
- 2 tbsp. raw sugar
- Zest, fresh grated from 1 medium lemon

For the topping:

- ¾ cup oats
- ⅓ cup vegan margarine
- 11/2 cups + 1 tbsp. whole wheat flour
- ½ cup raw sugar

Instructions:

1. If you are using coconut oil that is in liquid form, put it in the refrigerator for about 15 minutes until has the consistency of soft butter.
2. Preheat your oven to 400° F.
3. To start, mix all of the topping ingredients together in a bowl and refrigerate.
4. Chop the fruit for the crumble and toss into a saucepan over low heat together with the sugar, cinnamon, and lemon. Simmer until the fruit has softened.
5. Pour the crumble into a baking dish and finish with the crumble topping. Put in the oven for about 25 minutes. Enjoy!

Caramel Pecan Ice Cream

This is another ice cream recipe. However, this is a bit more complicated than the first one, but a must-have if you plan to entertain a big group at home or just put together something that your kids can regularly dip into throughout the summer months. Enjoy!

Yield: 6 servings

Ingredients:

For the ice cream:

- 1 quart vegan vanilla ice cream, softened
- ½ cup oats
- ½ cup brown sugar
- ¾ cups + 2 tbsp. whole wheat flour
- ½ cup coconut oil
- ½ cup pecans, chopped
- ¾ cup caramel sauce (the recipe is also included see below)

For the caramel sauce:

- ½ cup vegan margarine
- 1 cup brown sugar
- 1 tsp. cornstarch
- 1 tsp. vanilla

Instructions:

1. Start by preparing the caramel sauce. Melt the margarine in a small saucepan, then slowly stir in the sugar and vanilla until the mixture is smooth and everything is dissolved. Add the cornstarch and continue stirring until it is evenly distributed. Simmer the mixture until you get about a cup of caramel sauce.
2. For the ice cream, start by preheating your oven to 400° F.
3. In a large bowl, mix the flour, oats, sugar, and pecans. Add the coconut oil and mix thoroughly until evenly distributed.
4. In a baking pan, spread the mixture into a thin layer and bake for about 15 minutes. Stir every 5 minutes. Once done, crumble the mixture and allow it to cool down.
5. Put half of the crumb mixture into an 8×8 baking dish and drizzle half of the caramel sauce on top. Repeat this with the remaining crumble and caramel sauce mixture. Cover the dish with foil or a lid and refrigerate for an hour before cutting into squares.
6. Enjoy!

Tofu Sandwich

This is a great sandwich if you want to pack a healthy snack or lunch for your kids. Simply prepare this sandwich the morning before and your kids are taken cared of for the whole day.

Yield: 2 sandwiches

Ingredients:

- 2 slices tofu
- lettuce
- 2 tomato slices
- 2 avocado slices
- 2 slices vegan bread
- vegan mayonnaise
- vegan margarine
- vegetable oil
- salt and pepper

Instructions:

1. In a frying pan over medium heat, put the oil and cook the tofu on both sides until it is slightly brown. Season the tofu with salt and pepper.
2. Put together the sandwich according to your preference. Use as much margarine, mayonnaise and veggies as you feel necessary.
3. You can also grill the bread lightly before putting together the sandwich.

Mac and Cheese

Every kid loves a good mac and cheese. Now you know how to make one that's healthy too!

Yield: 2 servings

Ingredients:

- 8-oz macaroni noodles, cooked
- 1 ¾ cups soy milk
- ¼ cup nutritional yeast
- 1 tbsp. cornstarch
- 2 tbsp. light miso paste
- ¾ cup cashew nuts, raw
- ¼ cup canola oil
- 1 tbsp. lemon juice
- ½ tsp. garlic powder
- 1 tsp. onion powder
- ½ tsp. salt
- pinch of pepper

Instructions:

1. Finely grind the cashews using a food processor. You want to have a dust-like consistency for this. Once done, set the cashews aside.
2. In a saucepan, combine the milk, with the cornstarch and oil. Start with high heat until boiling, and then turn to low heat and simmer for about 10 minutes or until the cornstarch fully dissolves. To this mixture, add the ground cashew, miso paste, lemon juice, nutritional yeast, onion and garlic powder, and salt. Mix well. This will form your cheese mixture.
3. Pour the cheese mixture on the macaroni noodles and serve.

Macadamia Macaroons

This is another dessert that your kids are guaranteed to love for many years. Macadamia-flavored macaroons with a dark chocolate exterior; seriously, what's not to love?

Yield: 2 dozen macaroons

Ingredients:

- ⅓ cup whole wheat flour
- 2.5 cups desiccated coconut, unsweetened
- ½ cup macadamia nuts, chopped
- ½ cup coconut milk
- ⅓ cup agave nectar
- 1 small pinch salt
- 1 tsp. vanilla extract
- 100 g dark chocolate, melted

Instructions:

1. Preheat your oven to 350° F.
2. Line a baking tray with parchment paper.
3. In a large bowl, mix the flour, macadamia, coconut, coconut milk, agave, salt and vanilla extract.
4. Scoop out portions of the dough (it will be sticky) and put into the lined baking tray. To prevent the scoops from sticking, dip the scoop in cold water between scoops.
5. Bake for about 15 minutes or until the macaroons are lightly browned.
6. Allow the macaroons to cool, then dip in melted chocolate and put in the freezer for about 15 minutes to allow the coating to harden.
7. Enjoy!

Vegan Sugar Cookies

These are another great dessert that your kids will take a liking to almost as soon as they taste it. In addition, these are quite easy to prepare and pack, so there's plenty of reason for these to become a common fixture in your home. Try it out and see how the little ones respond.

Yield: 36 cookies

Ingredients:

For the sugar cookies:

- 1 cup margarine
- 3 ¾ cup all-purpose flour
- 1 cup white sugar
- 2 tsp. baking powder
- ½ cup applesauce (or other egg substitute)
- ¼ cup tofu cream cheese
- 1 tsp. vanilla extract

For the vegan icing:

- 2 cups confectioner sugar
- ½ tsp. almond extract
- 6-8 tsp. soy milk
- Vegan food coloring (color of your preference)
- 4 tsp. light corn syrup

Instructions:

1. For the sugar cookies, mix the margarine and sugar in a bowl. Continue mixing while adding in the vanilla extract and applesauce. Add the baking powder, flour, and tofu cream cheese.
2. Form the dough into a loaf and wrap in cellophane. Refrigerate the dough for two hours.
3. Meanwhile, preheat your oven to 350° F. Coat cookie sheets with a non-stick foil.
4. Take out the dough and on a surface with a light dusting of flour, roll it out to about ¼ inches in thickness. Using cookie cutters, cut into your desired shape and place on the cookie sheets.

5. Bake the cookies for about 12 minutes. Remove the cookies when done and allow to cool down. Store the cookies in an airtight container and refrigerate to allow the cookies to harden.

6. For the sugar icing, mix the confectioner sugar and soy milk in a medium bowl until smooth. Add the corn syrup and almond extract until the icing has a glossy texture. If necessary, use the corn syrup to thin down the icing. Add the food coloring of your choice.

7. Dip the cookies and allow to dry, preferably overnight.

Breakfast Cookies

Here's a breakfast option for your kids. Serve them these breakfast cookies with a glass of soy milk. It's healthy and filling too! What's not to love?

Yield: 2 dozen cookies

Ingredients:

- 11/2 cups rolled oats
- 2 bananas, ripe
- ⅔ cup applesauce
- ⅓ cup peanut butter
- ¼ cup maple syrup
- 1 tsp. vanilla
- 1 tsp. cinnamon
- ¼ cup walnuts
- ¼ cup raisins

Instructions:

1. Preheat your oven to 350° F.
2. Mash the banana into a paste-like consistency, then add the applesauce, maple syrup, peanut butter, cinnamon, and vanilla. Add the oats, nuts and raisins and mix well.
3. Line a cookie sheet with parchment paper and use a spoon to scoop and drop cookies on to the sheet. Bake for about 20 minutes and allow to cool down before serving.

Blueberry Macadamia Crumble

This crumble combines two great flavors: a macadamia crust with a blueberry filling! Check it out and see just how much your kids will love this great breakfast recipe. It even works as a dessert.

Yield: 8 servings

Ingredients:

For the blueberry filling:

- 2 cups fresh blueberries
- 2 tsp. lemon zest
- ¼ cup raw sugar
- 2 tsp. water

For the topping:

- ⅔ cup oats
- ⅔ cup whole wheat flour
- ½ cup raw sugar
- ¼ tsp. salt
- ½ cup coconut oil
- ¼ cup macadamia nuts, chopped

Instructions

1. If you are using liquefied coconut oil, put it inside the refrigerator for about 15 minutes to allow it to harden to the consistency of butter.
2. Preheat your oven to 375° F.
   While the coconut oil is in the refrigerator, mix all of the filling ingredients together and then pour over a baking dish or into small ramekins.
3. In a separate bowl, mix the flour, sugar, oats, and salt together. Add the coconut oil and continue mixing until the topping is even.
4. Pour the mixture over the filling and bake for about 30 minutes.

Pineapple Carrot Muffins

Here's a healthy muffin recipe that you can prepare any day of the week and is a sure-fire way to whet your kids' appetite.

Yield: 12 muffins

Ingredients

- 11/2 cups whole wheat flour
- 1 cup pineapple with juice, crushed
- 1 tsp. cinnamon
- 1 tsp. baking powder

- 1 tsp. baking soda
- ¼ cup brown sugar
- 1 cup carrots, grated
- ½ tsp. salt
- ¼ cup walnuts, chopped
- ¼ cup applesauce (or other egg substitute)
- 1 cup raw sugar
- ⅔ cup vegetable oil
- 1 tsp. vanilla

Instructions:

1. Mix the flour, baking soda, baking powder, cinnamon, and salt.
2. In a separate bowl, add the applesauce, sugar, oil and vanilla. To this wet mixture, add the dry mixture, including the pineapple and carrot chunks. Make sure that you chop the pineapple and carrots to the appropriate size.
3. Pour the mixture into muffin cups until each is about ¾ full.
4. Combine the brown sugar and nuts for the topping and sprinkle over the muffins.
5. Bake at 350 F for about 25 minutes and serve.

Vegan Meatballs

How about some sumptuous vegan meatballs? This is one of those recipes that will make your kids fall in love with the meatballs without them even knowing that there's no meat in the dish. This is perfect for lunch, dinner or anytime your kids need a good hearty meal. Enjoy!

Yield: 2 dozen meatballs

Ingredients

For the tomato sauce:

- 4 cans Italian-style tomatoes, peeled, drained
- ⅛ tsp. red chili pepper, crushed
- 8 medium garlic cloves, minced
- 2 tsp. olive oil
- ½ tsp. sugar
- 2 small onions
- ¼ tsp. Italian seasoning

- ¾ tsp. dried oregano
- salt

For the meat balls:

- 2⅔ cups vegetable broth
- 2 cups baby bella mushrooms, finely chopped
- ¾ cup rice, uncooked
- 1 cup bread crumbs, dried
- 4 tsp. olive oil
- 1 onion, diced
- ¼ cup applesauce (or other egg substitute)
- ¼ cup fresh parsley, chopped
- ⅓ cup almond/yeast mix
- 1 tsp. salt
- ½ tsp. pepper, freshly ground

Instructions:

For the tomato sauce:

1. In a large bowl, crush the tomatoes using a hand-blender. You can also use a blender.
2. In a pot over medium heat, put the oil and then sauté the onions and garlic until soft. This will take about 2 minutes. Toss in the oregano, red chilli pepper, and Italian seasoning. Cook for about 30 seconds, stirring continuously. Add the crushed tomatoes with the sugar and simmer. Flavor with salt and reduce the heat to low. Continue cooking for up to 45 minutes to thicken the mixture.

For the meat balls:

1. Heat the broth over high heat in a saucepan, then add the rice and reduce the heat to simmer uncovered. Cook until the rice is tender and the mixture is now creamy. This takes about 20 minutes. To prevent the rice from sticking, stir constantly for the last 5 minutes. Transfer the contents to a large bowl.
2. Pulse the mushrooms in batches using a food processor. You want the mushrooms to be finely chopped.
3. In a skillet, add the olive oil over medium-high heat and sauté the onions until translucent. This will take about 2 to 3 minutes. Continue cooking, adding the mushrooms until they are tender and most of the liquid has evaporated. This will take another 5 minutes. Toss the mixture in the bowl with rice and cool.
4. Preheat your oven to 400 F. Spray a baking sheet with cooking spray.

5. Mix the applesauce, almond/ yeast mix, breadcrumbs, parsley, salt and pepper to the rice mixture and mix well. Using your hands, form oval-shaped nuggets or round-shaped meatballs about 1.5 inches in diameter.

6. In another skillet, heat the remaining olive oil over medium heat and lightly fry the nuggets or meatballs until brown. Finish by putting the nuggets onto the baking sheet and then inside the oven for about 20 minutes.

7. Prepare your vegan pasta separately. Serve like you would any other meatball sauce. Enjoy!

Caramel Apple Muffins

This is another muffin recipe, but you can never have enough muffin recipes in your arsenal. If your kids love muffins, you'd adore these as the occasional alternative to your muffin line-up.

Yield: 12 muffins

Ingredients:

For the muffins:

- 1 3/4 cup all-purpose flour
- ¾ cup rolled oats, quick-cooking
- ¾ tsp. baking soda
- 1 apple, peeled, cored, diced
- 1 ¾ tsp. baking powder
- ¾ cup soy milk
- 1 tsp. cinnamon
- ¾ cup vegetable oil
- ⅔ cup brown sugar
- ¼ tsp. salt
- ¼ cup applesauce (or other egg substitute)
- 1 tsp. vanilla

For the topping:

- ¼ cup whole wheat flour
- 2 tbsp. vegan margarine, melted
- ⅓ cup brown sugar
- ⅓ cup pecans, chopped
- 1 tsp. cinnamon

Instructions:

1. For the topping, mix all of the ingredients thoroughly and set aside.
2. For the muffin, whisk the all-purpose flour and whole wheat flour in large bowl and then add the oats, cinnamon, baking powder, baking soda, and salt. This will form your dry mixture.
3. For the wet mixture, mix the soy milk with the oil, applesauce, vanilla and sugar. Pour the dry mixture into the wet mixture and mix thoroughly. Add the apple and blend, making sure not to over-mix.
4. Line your muffin cups with paper and pour the mixture up to the three-quarters level. Sprinkle the topping and bake in an oven preheated to 350° F for about 25 minutes.
5. Allow to cool down before serving. If stored in an airtight container, the muffins should last for up to 2 weeks.

Baked Oatmeal

You will love this great breakfast recipe. Not only is it easy to prepare, but it is also a healthy meal that's perfect to kick-start your kids' mornings!

Yield: 8 servings

Ingredients:

- 3 cups oats
- ½ cup sugar
- ½ tsp. salt
- 2 tsp. baking powder
- 1 tsp. cinnamon
- ½ cup raisins
- 6 tbsp. applesauce, unsweetened
- ½ cup oil
- 1 cup soy milk
- margarine (for greasing baking dish)

Instructions:

1. Preheat your oven to 350 degrees F. Meanwhile, grease a glass casserole dish with margarine.
2. Stir all the dry ingredients together in a bowl, then add the wet ingredients and mix well. Pour the mixture into the casserole dish and bake for about 35 minutes. Serve warm.

Vegan Homemade Fries

If your kids are like any other kids, they are in love with fries. Every time you pass by a fast-food chain, there's a pretty decent chance they'll be begging you for a quick stop and a serving or two of fries to boot. Now, you have an option.

Make them love the right kind of fries with this homemade vegan fries that they will surely love!

Yield: 3 servings

Ingredients:

- 3 large potatoes, chopped into 1/2 -inch squares
- 1 onion, diced
- 2 cloves garlic, minced
- 3 tbsp. olive oil
- 1/4 tsp. paprika
- 2 green onions, diced
- salt and pepper, to taste

Instructions:

1. Sauté the onion and garlic in the olive oil for about 5 minutes, then drop in the potato quarters and cook until tender. Make sure to stir frequently so that it browns evenly.
2. Drop the remaining ingredients into the pan and cook for about 3 more minutes.
3. Serve warm. You can also prepare vegetarian yogurt as a dip.

Vegan Apple Pie

Everyone loves a great apple pie. Make this your go-to recipe and share with your kids the joy of home-cooking a great pie today.

Yield: 8 servings

Ingredients:

For the filling:

- 5 organic apples, medium size
- 1/3 cup vegan margarine
- 1 tbsp. cinnamon

- 1/3 cup brown sugar
- 1 tbsp. nutmeg

For the crust:

- 4 cups flour
- ½ cup ice water
- 2 tsp. salt
- 1 1/3 cup + 2 tbsp. soy margarine

Instructions:

1. Prepare the crust first. Sift the dry ingredients first, then slowly mix small chunks of margarine into the mixture. Pour the cold water and continue mixing.
2. Split the dough into two balls. One will be for the bottom crust and the other for the top. Flatten the first one with a rolling pin. Check to make sure that the dough is not sticky and add flour accordingly, if necessary. You want to create a circular dough shape about 2 inches bigger in diameter than your pie pan. Neatly arrange the dough so that it covers the bottom of the pan. Press it down around the edges to make a pattern as you would commonly see in many local pies.
3. Preheat your oven to 350 degrees F.
4. Now, prepare the filling. Start by peeling the apples, then slice them thinly. In a bowl, mix the apple slices with the cinnamon, nutmeg and brown sugar. Pour the apple mixture into the pie crust, then cover the whole filling with the second dough using the same steps as indicated before. Use a butter knife to carefully cut ventilation holes in the center of the pie.
5. Bake the pie for about 45 minutes. Enjoy!

Cinnamon-Raisin Bread

Everyone loves a good piece of bread, especially if it's a cinnamon and raisin bread. Here's one recipe to tickle your kids' fancy and make them eat a healthy and filling meal.

Yield: 1 loaf

Ingredients:

- ¾ cup water
- 1 tbsp. margarine
- ¾ tsp. cinnamon, ground
- 2 cups bread flour
- ½ cup raisins

- 2 tsp. yeast
- 2 tbsp. granulated sugar
- ½ tsp. salt

Instructions:

1. You should have at least some ideas on how to make bread, right? Start off by tossing all the dry ingredients together until they are mixed well. Put all of the dry ingredients in a pile and then make a hole in the middle. Pour in the wet ingredients and start mixing thoroughly until you have a soft dough. Make sure not to overwork the dough.
2. Bake in a 300° F oven for about 20 minutes or until it turns golden brown.
3. Allow the bread to cool on a wire rack before serving.

Banana Bread

While we're at it, here's another bread recipe, this time made from bananas. Banana bread is deceptively simple to make and is always a hit with the kids. Make one that can last for up to a week so you'll have a ready snack available when your kids have cravings after a long day at school or at the playground.

Yield: 1 loaf

Ingredients:

- 1 ½ cups flour
- 3 ripe bananas, mashed
- ½ tsp. baking soda
- ½ tsp. baking powder
- ½ cup wheat germ
- 1 tbsp. lemon juice
- ½ cup oil
- ½ cup sweetener
- ¾ cup dates, chopped
- ½ tsp. salt

Instructions:

1. Preheat oven to 375F.

2. In a bowl, mix the mashed bananas with the lemon juice, sweetener, oil, and dates. Mix thoroughly.

3. In a separate bowl, mix the flour, salt, wheat germ, baking powder, and baking soda. Pour in the banana mixture into the flour mixture and mix well. Pour into a lightly oiled loaf pan and bake for about 45 minutes.

Vegan Blueberry Muffins

You can never have enough muffin recipes. Oh wait, did I already say that? Yes, you can never have enough muffin recipes in your arsenal and this is more proof that one more recipe can prepare you for the times when your kids just want something new! Cheers!

Yield:

Ingredients:

- 2 cups all-purpose flour
- 1/3 cup vegetable oil
- 1 + ½ tsp. baking soda
- 1 tsp. lemon extract
- ½ tsp. salt
- 1 tbsp. white vinegar
- lemon zest, freshly grated (from 2 lemons)
- 1 cup sugar
- 1 cup soy milk
- 1 + ½ cup blueberries

Instructions:

1. Preheat your oven to 375F and lightly grease muffin tins.
2. In a bowl, combine the flour with the baking soda, salt and lemon zest.
3. In another bowl, combine the milk, sugar, oil, extract, and vinegar. Mix well.
4. Add the dry ingredients to the wet ingredients stirring until fully combined. Be sure not to over-stir.
5. Drop in the berries and mix by gently folding using a rubber spatula.
6. Fill the muffin tins about 2/3 full, and bake for about 20 minutes.
7. Let the muffins cool on a wire rack for 5 minutes, then remove the muffins from the tins and continue cooling for another 15 minutes.

Vegan Coffee Cake

This doesn't fit the bill of common things your children will be craving on a daily basis but you to have to admit, this is a can't-miss vegan cake recipe. In some sense, this might be more for you than for your little ones, but hey, if you can sneak in a guilty pleasure while still ensuring that it's healthy, then why not?

Yield: 1 cake

Ingredients:

For the topping:

- 21/2 cups all-purpose flour
- 1 cup vegan butter, melted
- 1 cup brown sugar
- 11/2 tsp. cinnamon

For the cake:

- 3 cups all-purpose flour
- 1 cup vanilla almond milk
- ½ cup applesauce (or other egg substitute)
- 1 cup granulated sugar
- 5 tsp. baking powder
- ¼ cup vegetable oil
- 1 tsp. salt
- 4 tbsp. warm water
- 1 tbsp. + ½ tsp. vanilla extract

Instructions:

1. Preheat your oven to 325 F and oil a standard round spring form pan for the cake, then set aside.
2. First, prepare the topping. Melt the butter and then set aside to cool.
3. In a bowl, mix the brown sugar with the flour and cinnamon. Once combined, pour the melted butter into the bowl and continue mixing until the topping has an even consistency. Set aside.
4. For the cake, mix the applesauce with water in a blender or food processor until you get a good mixture, then set aside.

5. In another bowl, mix the flour with the granulated sugar, baking powder and salt. This will be your dry ingredient mix. For the wet ingredient mix, use a different bowl to whisk together ¼ cup applesauce (or other egg substitute), almond milk, oil and vanilla.

6. Pour all the dry ingredients onto a floured surface, then make a hole in the middle. Pour the wet ingredients into it and mix welt making sure not to over-mix.

7. Pour the cake batter into the pan and spread evenly. Top the cake mixture with the topping and bake for about 60 minutes.

Note: You can also make a blueberry version by putting dry blueberries on top of the cake mixture before pouring in the crumb topping.

Banana Bread Breakfast Pudding

Here's a slight tweak to your banana bread; instead of making the same bread every time, try making banana bread breakfast pudding instead!
It's easy and healthy too!

Yield: 1 serving

Ingredients:

- ½ ripe banana, mashed
- 3 tbsp. chia seeds
- ½ tsp. vanilla extract
- 1 tbsp. cocoa powder
- 1 tsp. coconut oil, melted
- ¼ cup vanilla rice milk

Instructions:

1. This is perhaps the easiest pudding recipe you will ever prepare in your life. Start by mashing the banana in a bowl, then adding the chia seeds. Mix well and continue adding the vanilla and cocoa. Stir together with coconut oil and vanilla rice milk.

2. Chill before serving!

Mint Chocolate Chip Cookies

Yield: 12 cookies

Ingredients:

- ¾ cup flour
- ½ tsp. baking soda
- ½ tsp. baking powder
- ½ cup cocoa powder, unsweetened
- ½ cup margarine
- ¾ cup sugar
- ¼ tsp. salt
- 1 tbsp. cornstarch
- 2 tbsp. water
- ½ cup vegan mint chocolate chips
- 1 tsp. vanilla

Instructions:

1. Preheat your oven to 350 degrees F and lightly grease a cookie sheet.
2. Mix all the dry ingredients together in a bowl.
3. In a coffee mug, dissolve the cornstarch into the water thoroughly until there are no more lumps.
4. Pour the cornstarch water together with the margarine and vanilla to the dry ingredients and mix until you have a soft dough
5. Separate into the desired cookie size and lay on the cookie sheet.
6. Bake for about 12 minutes and allow to cool on the cookie sheet before removing.
7. Serve with soy milk or your kids' favorite vegan milk.

Ultimate Vegan Brownies

If somebody ever tells you that they don't like vegan recipes because it's not decadent enough, give them this. Enough said!

Yield: 12 cookies

Ingredients:

- 1 cup coconut oil
- 1 cup pastry flour
- 1 tsp. baking powder

- 1 tsp. baking soda
- 1 cup whole wheat flour
- 4 oz. dark chocolate
- 1 tsp. vanilla
- ½ cup hot water
- 2 cups sugar
- 2 tsp. instant coffee
- ¾ cup cocoa
- 1 tsp. salt
- 2 tbsp. flax seeds, ground
- 6 tbsp. hot water

Instructions:

1. Preheat your oven to 350°F and grease an 8 x 8 baking pan.
2. Melt the coconut oil, chocolate and vanilla together in a bowl set over gently simmering water.
3. Mix the coffee with half a cup of hot water and pour in the melted chocolate mixture. Add the sugar and remove the bowl from the heat.
4. In a separate bowl, mix your dry ingredients together. The two flour types, cocoa, baking powder, baking soda and salt should combine thoroughly.
5. In a third bowl, mix the flax seeds with six tablespoons of hot water and let it sit for about 3 minutes.
6. Now, it all comes together. Pour the melted chocolate mixture into the flour mixture and stir to make a batter. Continue building the batter by adding the thickened flax and stir.
7. Gently pour the batter into the greased baking pan and bake for about 40 minutes.
8. Once cooked, remove the brownies from the oven and cool on a rack. Serve the brownies at room temperature to get the best texture.

Homemade Veggie Dogs

Veggie hotdogs! Seriously, that's all your kids need to hear before they come scrambling to the kitchen for a great meal. Of course, you can politely emit the "veggie" part for better effect and these hot dogs will taste just as great!

Yield: 8 hotdogs

Ingredients:

- ½ medium onion, coarsely chopped

- 3 cloves garlic
- ¾ cup pinto beans, cooked, well-drained
- ½ cup + 2 tbsp. water
- 2 tbsp. soy sauce
- 1 tbsp. tomato paste
- 2 tsp. paprika, smoked
- 1 tsp. coriander, ground
- 1 tsp. mustard, ground
- ½ tsp. black pepper
- ¼ tsp. celery seed
- ¼ tsp. mace
- salt
- 1 cup vital wheat gluten
- 1/3 cup oatmeal, rolled, uncooked
- 2 tbsp. nutritional yeast
- 1 tbsp. flax seeds, ground

Instructions

1. Mix the onion and garlic in a food processor and pulse to chop finely.
2. In a non-stick skillet, sauté the onion and garlic until softened. This takes about 3 minutes.
3. Put the onion mixture back in the food processor and add the pinto beans, water, soy sauce, tomato paste, and all seasoning. Blend the mixture again until you get a thin paste.
4. In a large bowl, toss together the gluten, flax, oatmeal, and yeast and pour the mixture into the food processor. Pulse again until thoroughly combined.
5. Put a steamer on top of a pot of water which you will bring to a boil.
6. Prepare 8 pieces of aluminum foil about 6 inches long and divide the gluten into 8 equal pieces. Roll a piece of gluten between the palms of your hands until you have a rough hotdog shape, then place it on the foil and roll up. Twist both ends to close and repeat for the remaining 7 hotdogs.
7. Place all the veggie dogs on the steamer, cover, and cook with steam for about 45 minutes.
8. Once done, remove from the heat and allow to cool before unwrapping. Store the veggie dogs in a covered container in the refrigerator.
9. Serve by frying or warming in a microwave.

Conclusion

It is never easy to convince your kids to go the vegan way. Between the temptations, the misconceptions, and the peer pressure, not to mention the likely taste factor if you're running out of options in the kitchen, then it will most likely be a hard fight every meal until you can convince them to eat what's on the table.

However, it's never fun if you need to prepare to separate meals for you and your kids. After a long day at work, the last thing you need is cook two different dishes so that you and the kids can get what you want.

We hope that you'll never have to deal with this situation again. With these kid-friendly vegan recipes, we know that you now have more than enough firepower to catch their attention and serve them healthy vegan meals without their knowledge.

Cheers in the kitchen. Practice. Cook and experiment!

We know that this book will put you on the road to becoming a great vegan cook, and one that your kids will love more than the next fast-food chain down the street!

Printed in Great Britain
by Amazon